MW00930665

This Notebook Belongs To:

____

Made in the USA
Las Vegas, NV
26 February 2021

18671437R00069